# Lionel Conacher

Frank Cosentino and Don Morrow

Fitzhenry & Whiteside Limited

# Lionel Conacher

## Contents

© 1981 Fitzhenry & Whiteside Limited
150 Lesmill Road, Don Mills, Ontario M3B 2T5

*Editor* Cathleen Hoskins
*Designer* Susan Budd

Printed and bound in Canada by
T. H. Best Printing Company Limited

**The Canadians** A continuing series
*General Editor* Robert Read
*Consulting Editor* Roderick Stewart
*Series Editor* Rosalind Sharpe

To all the "Little Trains" in Canada
and
To Mrs. Victoria Mayhue

Cosentino, Frank, 1937-
   Lionel Conacher

(The Canadians)

Includes index.
Bibliography: p.

ISBN 0-88902-679-3

1. Conacher, Lionel, 1900-1954.  2. Athletes —
Canada — Biography.  I. Morrow, Don.  II.
Series.

GV697.C66C67     796'.092'4     C80-094807-6

# The Uphill Climb Chapter 1

May 24, 1900, was a day of celebration across Canada. It was Queen Victoria's birthday, a time for festivities throughout the thirty-three-year-old Dominion. In the city of Toronto every public and high school held ceremonies in honour of the monarch's eighty-first birthday. The entire city was decorated with Union Jack flags and festive bunting. In a corner of the north end of the city, at 92 Davenport Road, there was still another reason to celebrate. A son was born that day to Benjamin and Elizabeth Conacher. Christened Lionel Pretoria, he was the oldest boy and third-born of ten children in the Conacher clan.

Mr. and Mrs. Conacher were proud working-class people. Ben Conacher could trace his ancestry back to the Duke of Rutland, a fact about which Lionel and his brothers and sisters were constantly reminded by their grandmother. The name Lionel was taken from a distant ancestor. His second name, Pretoria, suggested the Conachers' sense of patriotism and dedication to the British Empire. For some months prior to Lionel's birth,

*Thousands of flag-waving people jammed the streets of downtown Toronto to celebrate the end of the Boer War.*

the South African city of Pretoria was featured in the daily news as the target of British troops in their 1400-kilometre trek from Cape Town to the Boer capital. In honour of the inevitable British victory Mrs. Conacher added Pretoria to the name of her eldest son. (She also named one of her daughters Victoria after the great queen of England.)

Benjamin Conacher was a hard-working Scot, who met and courted Elizabeth Black, a young Irish immigrant working as a maid. They married in 1894 and settled in the working-class north end of Toronto. Davenport Road and Cottingham Square across from Jesse Ketchum Park and School were later described by Lionel's brother Charlie as "one of Toronto's higher class slums". Ben Conacher was a teamster, driving his horse and wagon to a variety of jobs in an effort to eke out a living. There were no luxuries in this family; each of the Conacher children was brought up knowing the harsh realities of a large family competing for its daily existence. But everyone in the family contributed as best he or she could and developed self-reliance in the process. Each child's formal schooling ended soon after grade eight; their "higher" education was in the school of hard knocks.

As the Conacher family grew at the turn of the twentieth century, Canada was calling to the world for settlers to develop the potentially wheat-rich Prairies. The eastern provinces also promised wealth and progress in mining and manufacturing. It was a period of optimism and prosperity, a time when Prime Minister Sir Wilfrid Laurier could boastfully claim that the twentieth century would be the century of Canada. As the century progressed, tremendous changes in transportation and communication were developed and refined for public use (the railroad, the telephone, the automobile, newspapers, wire services, the airplane and radio).

In almost every phase of life, change was the word of the day, and the field of sport was no exception. In fact, sport both reflected and contributed to the growth and changes in Canadian society. By the end of the nineteenth century organized sport was firmly planted in the country, and definite characteristics ruled Canadian sport at that time. Amateur sport was of chief importance. Up to 1884 the principles of amateurism had required that competition be limited to people who did not earn money doing physical labour. "Professionals" were those who did manual labour to earn a living, and these athletes were thought to have an unfair advantage in strength and endurance. This concept of amateurism effectively divided sport on the basis of social class, with the upper- and middle-class "amateurs" dominating sport at all levels. However, after 1884 a new notion of professionalism entered sport. From that time on a "professional" has been an athlete who is paid *to compete in sport.*

As Canada entered the twentieth century, new patterns emerged in sport and all areas of life. The effects of industrialism became more widespread, and more leisure time was available to a greater number of Canadians in all social classes. The British influence in Canada was tempered by that of the geographically closer United States, as well as by the cultures of European immigrants. In the late nineteenth century the main sports had been those of the English and Scottish immigrants — horse racing, cricket, curling and rowing.

*A popular local shop in the neighbourhood where Lionel Conacher grew up*

But in the early twentieth century there was a dramatic shift among participants and spectators towards North American team sports, such as lacrosse, football, baseball and hockey. Opportunities for participation in all kinds of sports filtered down to the working class, as commercialism and the new notion of professionalism took hold. In the early years of the twentieth century lacrosse, hockey and, to a certain extent, baseball were developed to a level of excellence that attracted paying crowds.

Team sports were naturally suited to mass spectatorship, mass advertising and mass marketing. Because of the decreased British influence and increased industrial and political connections with the United States, Canadian-American competition in sport grew stronger. American influences on Canadian sport were strengthened by radio programs, movies and theatre productions from the United States. The organization and playing of baseball, football, lacrosse and hockey in Canada gradually drew in line with the American model. Canada followed the United States in organizing sport from mass participation at the youth league level to elite professional competition at the top of the sport ladder. Spectators and athletes alike — indeed all of Canadian society — were attracted to the American systems of sport and almost everything else. It must be remembered, however, that American influence won Canadians through example rather than force. Canadians were eager to embrace American culture.

At the centre of this early twentieth-century development of Canadian sport stood Lionel Conacher. In his lifetime he excelled in Canadian sport, even dominated it. Sport shaped his life, his character, his physique. If the passion for participation in sport can be seen as a celebration of the human spirit, then Lionel Conacher may be viewed as an amazing example of that spirit.

Many factors contributed to Lionel's growth as an athlete. The Conacher home was a major influence. Though their income was quite modest, the Conachers were rich in love and moral support. It was said that Benjamin Conacher never raised his voice in anger at any of his children. The table was always filled with food, and every Sunday morning the children would be

*Benjamin Conacher, Lionel's father, was a teamster, like the man in this 1914 photograph.*

lined up in their clean, starched clothes to be given their money for the offering at the Church of the Redeemer a few blocks away. Elizabeth Conacher was a religious woman who set the rules of behaviour and discipline in the home. The children never considered that any other code of conduct or style of living could exist.

A typical day of winter work might take Ben Conacher to Centre Island to cut ice for summer use. To cover the eight kilometres from home to the foot of Toronto Bay, he left his house at five in the morning and arrived about seven, after walking across the frozen bay. Until evening he would cut squares of ice, storing them in the ice houses for the summer. At six o'clock it was time to start the two-hour trip home. He earned seven dollars and fifty cents per week for this work, but that was not enough to keep his growing family. During the winter he would pause only briefly at home to eat his supper before hitching a plough to his horse and cleaning the snow off the ice rinks at Jesse Ketchum

Park. The extra dollar he received each night helped to make ends meet.

During the summer Benjamin Conacher worked at various teamster jobs, and young Lionel always met his father at the end of the day. He enjoyed driving the team of horses to the stable. By 1912 Mr. Conacher's pay was averaging nine dollars per week and there were six children. One night twelve-year-old Lionel was busy helping unhitch the team when the boss asked his father to hire another man to help haul sod from the Don Valley. Lionel begged his father to let him do the job, saying over and over, "I can do it, I can do it." With some pride, the elder Conacher agreed.

The next morning at five, school conveniently set aside, young Lionel arose, drove a team to the Don Valley and loaded and delivered sod from eight until six. This long day of work proved that the boy *could* do it and, in addition, earned an extra dollar for the family!

Family, friends and hard work were all strong influences on young Lionel Conacher. But books also fuelled his active imagination and his determination to realize his dreams. At some point Lionel began to read the adventures of Burt L. Standish's fictional hero Frank Merriwell, a student at Yale University in Connecticut. Merriwell could do anything; he was the essence of youthful heroes. When all looked hopeless, Merriwell would save the girl from the villain, steal home with the winning run, score the tie-breaking goal or run for the winning touchdown. When the odds seemed impossible, it was time for a "Frank Merriwell finish". Conacher later said that the legendary exploits of Frank Merriwell set a great example for him.

Conacher was lucky that Jesse Ketchum School, which was close by, was in the hands of a principal who believed in the virtue of sport. At the Mimico Industrial School in 1903 William F. Kirk developed a theory that organized games would help develop a sense of discipline, pride, self-respect and initiative in boys who had run into trouble with the law. These boys were sent to reform schools such as Mimico, where they usually sat around in silent groups waiting to follow some natural leader. Kirk wisely organized the boys into team sports. He was pleased with his results at Mimico, and when he was appointed principal at Jesse Ketchum

*Title page of the 1904 edition of one of Lionel Conacher's favourite boyhood books*

# FRANK MERRIWELL'S RETURN TO YALE

BY

## BURT L. STANDISH

AUTHOR OF

"Frank Merriwell's Schooldays,"
"Frank Merriwell's Trip West,"
"Frank Merriwell's Chums,"
"Frank Merriwell's Foes,"
"Frank Merriwell Down South," etc.

PHILADELPHIA
DAVID McKAY, PUBLISHER,
604-8 SOUTH WASHINGTON SQUARE.

School in the city's tough north end, Kirk decided to introduce his scheme there too. Basing his system on one popular at many British public schools and Canadian private schools, Kirk insisted that every student participate in some organized sport. With some pupils the principal's plan had little success (Mickey MacDonald, at one time Canada's most wanted criminal, lived in the area), but for the Conachers, especially Lionel, Kirk's sport philosophy had vivid results.

Ted Reeve once wrote that "every kid in Cottingham Square or Jesse Ketchum Park played lacrosse, rugby and hockey, and you had to fight or move." Lionel and his brothers and sisters were no exception. Whenever they could take the time from school or chores, the Conacher children played games from morning to night, summer and winter. Lionel's brother Charles, nine years younger and himself destined to be a great athlete, later recalled:

*Lionel (at left) with a friend. This is the earliest known picture of Toronto's budding sports superstar.*

The Conachers got so involved in games that we had no time to think about, say, sticking up a bank. In the winter, we'd come home from school, put on our skates and rush back to the rink until suppertime. We wouldn't even take off our skates while we ate. We'd tramp into the kitchen through the back door, sit down and eat, and tramp back to the rink until they turned off the lights at nine o'clock.

Jesse Ketchum Park, with its open fields, two rinks and William Kirk's influence, was only three doors away on Davenport Road.

For the Conachers and their friends, however, the street was the arena for their favourite pastime, road hockey. Even on hot summer days they would use a sponge ball for a puck and old coal sacks for goals. Occasionally, they would stage a formal street line-up for a mouth organ rendition of "God Save the King". The coal sacks served a dual purpose. The game was played on the street next to a coal yard. The signal for the end of the game was to fire the ball deep into the yard. The players would rush in to search for the ball, carrying the "goal posts" with them. The ball was always found — as well as a few chunks of coal for the family stove!

The Conacher family was certainly poor, but among others from the same neighbourhood their poverty was seldom noticeable. At Christmas time youngsters in the neighbourhood often wore identical sweaters, mitts and toques, all gifts from the *Toronto Daily Star* Santa Claus fund and the local Church of the Redeemer.

It soon became obvious to Lionel Conacher that one of the ways to "rise above the blunted cornerstones of Davenport Road" was through excellence in sport. He repeatedly told his brother, "If you want to live better, Charlie, you've got to make good at something, and I don't know where we're going to do it if it isn't in sports."

Sports in the Conacher family really started with Dorothy, the oldest child. Neither parent had any athletic background, but Dorothy won races at picnics and playgrounds, and the prizes and praise she received impressed young Lionel. For many years Lionel and Dorothy had to convince their parents, who had always had to work from daybreak to dusk, that they should be involved in sport. Their parents felt the time could be put to better use contributing to family chores. Judging by the athletic skills of the Conacher children, Lionel's and Dorothy's pleas and examples must have convinced the parents of the value of sport. Dorothy, Mary, Victoria and the female twins, Nora and Kay, were all good skaters and softball players during their adolescence. Charlie's success in professional hockey with the Toronto Maple Leafs was such that he is still credited with the fastest shot in the history of the sport. The twin brothers, Roy and Bert, were both good hockey players, and Roy played for several teams during his ten-year National Hockey League career, winning the scoring championship one season and being named to the All-Star team another. The youngest brother, Dermott, played football for a few years but did not continue in sports.

Lionel Conacher's first venture into the world of sports, except for road hockey, occurred in the summer of 1913. Dressed in old clothes, he wandered over to a neighbourhood playground where a pick-up game of rugby football was in progress. Conacher knew nothing of the rules, and he was much less skilled than the other thirteen-year-olds. However, the young, lean youth had a "soul-consuming desire . . . above all to emulate the great Frank Merriwell of fiction." He was beginning to feel the surge of developing physical strength, and he later recalled, "I longed in every bit of me to achieve that state of physical prowess where I could rise upon demand to great heights."

The young athlete soon began to explore a variety of sports offered at a number of small sports clubs and locations in Toronto. At Queen Elizabeth playground he was introduced to baseball. Somewhat further from Conacher's neighbourhood the Capitals lacrosse team operated a fifty-two-kilogram feeder team at Kew Gardens. Everywhere he played, the fourteen-year-old Conacher impressed everyone with determination far beyond his years and size. Consequently, Lionel became a good prospect for many teams and sporting organizations. At homemade gyms and the Central YMCA Lionel took up boxing and wrestling. In 1916 he won the sixty-one-kilogram wrestling championship of Ontario and in 1920, the light heavyweight boxing championship of Canada. As a twelve-year-old he had joined the Century Rovers hockey club. Though he had an awkward skating style and was discouraged from playing hockey because of the expense of skates and other equipment, Lionel continued to be enthusiastic about the game. At age sixteen he joined the hockey team sponsored by the Aura Lee Club, a neighbourhood

*Baseball, hockey, wrestling, football, lacrosse — young Lionel Conacher excelled in every sport he played.*

organization with which he was associated for the rest of his teenage years.

Obviously, Conacher was an athlete blessed with a talent for sport. He probably could have made a name for himself in any of these sports. But it was in football that Lionel was to excel and to become nationally famous. He had been introduced to the game at a fairly early age and, more importantly, had all his equipment provided for him. Football soon became the central channel for the young athlete's skills. He joined the Capitals football team as a middle wing (tackle) in a forty-three-kilogram weight league. Lionel helped lead the team to the Toronto city championship in 1914. As Conacher grew and added weight to his large-boned body, his coach in 1919, Mike Rodden, experimented by switching Lionel from tackle on the line of scrimmage to backfield ball-carrier. In those days there was no such thing as blocking for the ball-carriers beyond the line of scrimmage. The player running with the ball relied totally upon his own skill to evade defensive players. It seemed to Rodden that Conacher's size, determination and speed made him perfect for running with the ball. The young powerhouse thrived in his new position.

By 1919 Lionel Conacher was recognized informally as the best all-round athlete in Toronto. In that year alone the two hockey teams he played for both won Canadian titles, and the Capitals captured the Ontario championship in football. At twenty years of age Conacher was the most sought-after athletic star in senior amateur sport in the Queen City. From that point he embarked on an athletic career unparalleled in the history of Canadian sport.

# The Big Train Chapter 2

Some have called the 1920s the Golden Age of Canadian Sport. Certainly, the Lionel Conacher legend began to flourish then. By 1920 he was a raw-boned 183 centimetres and weighed ninety-one kilograms. His teams were champions, and young Conacher was much in demand in the established amateur sports as well as in the increasingly acceptable professional sporting circles. During that year he helped the Parkdale Canoe Club win the Toronto junior hockey championships; he won the Canadian light heavyweight boxing championship, played baseball with Parkdale and led the Torontos to the Ontario Rugby Football Union championship.

By this time the Victorian era had faded into the background. World War I had exploded many conventions and attitudes of the late nineteenth century. New inventions, such as the automobile, radio and airplane, were rapidly changing people's lives. Ways that had been accepted for generations were being pushed aside by new attitudes, increased technology and social upheaval. Sport too had changed. The nineteenth-century concept of amateur athletics had shifted from restrictions based on social class to restrictions tied to money. One could not earn any amount of money playing a sport and still be labelled an "amateur". The governing body of sport, the Amateur Athletic Union of Canada, ruled that a person who was declared a professional (i.e., made money) in one sport was barred from playing any amateur sport.

This ruling was a powerful block against professionalism. Amateur sport still offered the best competition and training for the finest athletes. Most clubs in Canada started out as multi-sport organizations, encompassing sports such as football, lacrosse, hockey and rowing. Athletes who competed for a club moved from one sports season to the next, sharpening their various skills and usually being offered a position with a company belonging to a club member. Only in hockey, where the National Hockey League had developed and where professionals competed for the coveted Stanley

*Twenty-year-old Lionel Conacher*

*Who governs amateur sport in Canada today? Who governs professional sport? What powers do these organizations have?*

Cup, could an athlete make a fair living from sport. However, the professional hockey player gave up his opportunity to participate in any other sport. Once the hockey season ended (it usually ran from the end of October to the end of February, approximately twenty-four games), all amateur sports were denied to him.

Today, though almost all sports have gone professional, there is no chance for a professional player in one sport to compete in any other. Two main factors prevent the rise of multi-sport stars like Conacher. First, because of inventions such as artificial ice, professional sport seasons are now much longer. The seasons for sports such as baseball, football and hockey often overlap. Secondly, contracts for professional athletes now include clauses forbidding participation in any other sport (often including leisure activities, such as skiing) without the club's permission. These clauses are intended as safeguards against injuries. But during Conacher's career the amateur was still the norm, and outstanding athletes wanted to excel in more than one sport.

As Lionel mastered sport after sport, various clubs, organizations and individual promoters tried to attract the talented young athlete. At the same time he realized that as the oldest boy in a family of ten children he had to do something to help pay the bills at home. It became more and more obvious that sport was the answer. He enjoyed it, understood it and was persistent and talented enough to excel.

In general, clubs and players were careful to abide by the letter, if not the spirit, of the amateur code. Though an athlete was not officially being paid, he might find a ten- or twenty-dollar bill in his shoe at the end of a good game. In Lionel's case, he attracted a following of idolizing fans and "was catered to and fawned upon by men of considerable prominence in business and professional life." Sporting entrepreneurs, both professional and amateur, were businessmen always on the lookout for a new "phenom", a star who could attract the public and its money. The St. Pats, Toronto's entry in the new National Hockey League, offered the young Conacher $3000 to play the 1920-21 season with them. But the "Big Boy" turned down the offer (which was three times the average NHL salary) as well as the $500

*Bill Burch, Lionel Conacher's best friend from his Jesse Ketchum days*

cash bonus the eager team management flashed in front of him. The money certainly attracted young Lionel; but his advisers — coaches and businessman Harris Ardiel — convinced him that it was not in his best interests to "turn pro" and lose his chance to compete in other sports.

There were other ways around the money problem. Though Conacher could not be paid directly, jobs could be made available to him. As a twenty-year-old, Conacher was given a position with the Toronto-Dominion Bank. Harris Ardiel, a Toronto sportsman who had taken a liking to the young athlete and who was involved in many sporting organizations, made certain that Conacher and his friend, Billy Burch, were hired in return for their participation on various Toronto-Dominion teams. In the high-unemployment period after World War I a job was a powerful inducement.

There were other opportunities. A clothing salesman wanted to use the sporting reputation of Conacher and Burch to attract customers to his store. In return for salaries their names were put over the door and the two were on hand to greet customers. It proved to be a successful sales gimmick. Impressed by the venture, Conacher and Burch decided to establish their own business once the current agreement expired. A cleaning, dyeing and pressing business on Bloor Street flourished for two years, until Conacher moved from Toronto to Pittsburgh, Pennsylvania, in 1923.

Because Lionel Conacher was such an outstanding athlete in so many sports and because he often seemed to

*Conacher's business card in 1922*

CONACHER'S

Cleaning, Dyeing
and Pressing Service

Orders Called for and Delivered
to all Parts of the City.

*Call North 63*

45 BLOOR EAST

LIONEL CONACHER
PROPRIETOR
AND MANAGER

come through in legendary Frank Merriwell fashion, sportswriters soon dreamed up an amazing assortment of nicknames for him. The Blond Express, Iron Man, Athletic Superman, the Human Dynamo, Big Moose, Lion, Connie, Wonder Man of Canadian Athletics, Gargantuan Canuck, Canadian Youth of Herculean Stature, Muscular Mohican, the Mastodonic Form were all used to describe the powerful and capable Conacher. But no name identified him so accurately as the Big Train.

The name took root in the popular imagination. The idea of a powerful steam engine racing relentlessly to its destination was still a source of awe in the early part of the century. In the United States the New York baseball pitcher Walter Johnson was known by that name, and in Ontario, as early as 1909, a hard-charging ball carrier named Smirle Lawson was commonly referred to as the Big Train. In 1921 it was Lionel Conacher, the new Big Train, who roared to national prominence in Canada's premier football contest, the Grey Cup.

Football had always been Conacher's first love, but it was only after he was moved to the halfback position and began to carry the ball that the Big Train became famous. In 1921 Conacher left the Capitals to join Harris Ardiel's Argonauts. The press coverage surrounding the transfer brought Conacher into the limelight. Everyone seemed to recognize his name. For a big man, Conacher was extremely fast and tricky on his feet. But he was just as likely to plough in a straight line toward the goal line as he was to try to finesse his way around his opponents. Once he was in an open field, however, he had the speed to outrun just about everyone. In addition to Conacher, the Argonauts were blessed with the gifted Harry "Red" Batstone. Batstone was an outstanding athlete who paired well with Conacher. He was able to draw defenders towards him, then lateral the ball to Conacher, who would burst into the open for a touchdown. Toronto newspapers, such as the *World, Globe, Telegram, Daily Star* and *Mail*, tried to outdo each other in praise of Toronto's "dynamic duo". Batstone was the playmaker, but Conacher brought the crowd to its feet.

In his first game with the Argonauts in September 1921, Conacher scored twenty-three of twenty-seven points. From that moment the Toronto fans began to dream of a Grey Cup victory. Sportswriters reported that Conacher "had as much fun as a pickerel in a minnow pond." The size of the man and his awesome exploits seemed to beg for hyperbole and superlatives. His play against Hamilton was said to have "stood out like a red vest at a funeral." One writer ventured that defences would need "a gallon of Lepages to stop his gallops." Opponents who dared to derail the Big Train were said to have "wanted to get the *croix de rugby* for stopping the mightiest gridiron warrior in the broad Dominion."

*Conacher in the distinctive Argonaut football uniform. Note the shoulder pads worn outside the sweater.*

Conacher was the major factor in every Argonaut victory during the 1921 season, but he literally outdid himself in the Grey Cup game of that year. Though not the national celebration it is today, the Grey Cup had been the culmination of the "Dominion Championship" since 1909. And in 1921 the match had a special interest. It was the first occasion of an East-West showdown. The Eskimos from Edmonton made the long journey by train to meet the Argonauts. Trying to prepare his team for the big contest, Deacon White, the Edmonton coach, scouted the game between the Argos and the Parkdale Canoe Club. White, an American from Northwestern University, was obviously in awe of the Big Train:

> The teams would have been evenly matched had Conacher not been playing with the Argos. Say, he is a running fool — not tricky, but just runs like hell. He weighs about ten off two hundred and is six feet two inches — legs on him like an ox. If he can't get past a man he charges him. He made several forty- and fifty-yard runs, and booted the ball on a similar average.

Almost ten thousand spectators witnessed and thousands more read of Conacher's Grey Cup exploits. The Argonauts blanked the Eskimos 23-0. Conacher scored fifteen points on two touchdowns, a drop kick field goal and two single points, all in the first three quarters of the game. In what seems an incredible move today, Conacher actually left the Grey Cup match before it was over so that he could join his Aura Lee hockey teammates in a game against the Toronto Granites.

Football, which was Canada's most popular autumn sport, generated more and more publicity for the budding superstar. At the same time, however, Conacher continued to develop his talents in hockey. Early in his career he had relied on bulldozing rushes and direct shots at the goalie. But with each season he gained more skill and confidence. He was described as an excellent defenceman with "a wicked shot . . . always dead on for the corner."

Once again promoters tried to lure Conacher into the National Hockey League. This time Leo Dandurand of the Montreal Canadiens offered to pay Conacher $5000 and to establish him in business in Montreal. Again Conacher declined. Conacher sensed that his appeal was based more on his talents in other sports than on his abilities as a hockey player. But could Conacher afford to

*Lionel Conacher, c. 1922*

turn down such huge sums of money? Certainly, playing as an amateur would never make him rich.

During this time there had been charges challenging Conacher's amateur status and that of the Aura Lee hockey team. These had been investigated and dismissed by the Amateur Athletic Union of Canada. However, a Toronto-based periodical, *Sport*, re-opened the issue in August and September 1922. This time Conacher reacted swiftly with a $10 000 libel suit against the publishing company and the editor, E.J. (Eddy) Livingston. Livingston was a Toronto lawyer who owned the Torontos, the city's representative in the professional National Hockey Association (NHA). During World

War I troubles began developing between Livingston and other team owners in Montreal and Ottawa. The Montreal and Ottawa groups withdrew from the National Hockey Association and formed their own league, the National Hockey League (NHL), in 1917. They invited a new franchise, the Toronto St. Pats, to join them.

Livingston was furious and immediately tried to upstage the new league and its Toronto entry. He wanted to recruit Lionel Conacher for his team. When it became clear that Conacher was more interested in amateur hockey than either the NHL or the NHA, Livingston became convinced that the young athlete had to be taking money under the table. He set out to ruin the Conacher image. The charges and countercharges caused an uproar in the sports establishment, and Conacher launched his libel suit. The case was settled out of court, and a full apology from Livingston appeared in the Toronto newspapers on November 3, 1922.

The excitement over this incident can only be understood if we look at the young athlete's impressive activities during this period. In addition to his tremendous following as a football and hockey star, he had been described as "the greatest lacrosse player in the game". Chosen by the press for the 1922 All-Star team, Conacher was double-teamed, triple-teamed throughout the season. Sometimes a fresh opponent was put on him every quarter in a desperate attempt to stop him. Reports described him as "the bright light of the team", and his play was said to be "one of the greatest exhibitions ever seen in Toronto". When Conacher turned to start a rush and extended his arm "protectingly in a swerving dash for the goal", the result was described as a "sensation". Promoters swooped in to make the most of the public's fascination with Toronto's superstar:

**CONACHER**
**CANADA'S GREATEST ATHLETE**
**WILL PLAY IN THE**
**RIVERSIDE V. MAITLANDS**
**LACROSSE GAME**
**SCARBOROUGH BEACH**
**SATURDAY 3:15 P.M.**
**RAIN OR SHINE.**

*Conacher and a Maitlands teammate race for the ball during a field lacrosse game in the early 1920s.*

Conacher's other summer sport was baseball. From 1920 to 1923 the Toronto Maple Leafs baseball team tried to sign the young athlete to a contract. The Leafs, who played in the professional International League, knew that Conacher's baseball exploits and his wide popular appeal made him the most important new player they could add to their lineup. Conacher played a variety of positions — pitcher, catcher, fielder — but it was his batting power that thrilled the public. Known as a slugger, he frequently won games at the eleventh hour in typical Frank Merriwell fashion. His ability to slam the ball with a "terrific clout" while batting as high as .400 led teams including Detroit and Baltimore to make him offers sight unseen. It didn't take much imagination to recognize Conacher's potential as a drawing card.

Even in his own time Conacher's fame was legendary. In 1922 the popular heavyweight boxing champion Jack Dempsey was asked to box a four-round exhibition with the Big Train for the benefit of Christie Hospital in Toronto. Dempsey agreed. As a good-natured prank, Senator Frank O'Connor of the Laura Secord Candy Company offered Lionel $100 if he could give Dempsey "one on the chin". He did, causing the startled Jack Dempsey to scold the young upstart.

In 1924 Conacher performed one of his most famous feats. Baseball and lacrosse seasons coincided with each other. In June 1924 Conacher's baseball team, the Hillcrests, were losing by one run in the bottom of the last inning. With the bases loaded, Conacher hit a double to centre field to win the game. Calling a taxi, the "Iron Man" made his way to Scarborough Beach, where the Maitlands lacrosse team was losing 2-1 at half-time. Conacher scored two goals in the fourth quarter to lead his team to a 3-2 victory.

But it was the year 1923 that was pivotal in Conacher's career. Aware that his ability to play sport

*During Jack Dempsey's 1920 visit to Toronto, Conacher (third from right, holding hat) posed with Dempsey, Dempsey's manager and several local sportswriters. Have many Canadians become world-class boxers in this century?*

*The ice rink at Pittsburgh's Duquesne Gardens, home of the Pittsburgh Yellow Jackets*

would someday diminish and that the wear and tear and natural ageing of his body would eventually take their toll, he saw opportunity knocking from afar — on the hockey rinks of Pittsburgh, Pennsylvania. This opportunity was different from previous offers to play hockey with professional teams. This was amateur hockey; he would still be able to play other sports. And even more important was the opportunity to pursue his education and the chance to step into a ready-made career in insurance sales. It was too good to pass up.

A transplanted Torontonian, Roy Schooley, was manager of Pittsburgh's Duquesne Gardens, described as "the largest and most beautiful skating palace in the world". As a professional promoter, Schooley had been aware of the impression Lionel Conacher had made on hockey fans in Boston. The big, hard-charging defenceman had played exhibition games there with Aura Lee after the 1921 and 1922 seasons. In Canada the mere appearance of Conacher was enough to attract a multitude of spectators. For days prior to Conacher's

refereeing of a game between the Frontenacs and
Queen's University, the newspapers raved about his
upcoming appearance.

Schooley was also secretary of the United States
Amateur Hockey Association. Although professional
hockey had its North American beginnings in the United
States, amateur teams were more numerous and
powerful there. (The National Hockey League was to
play competitively in the United States for the first time
in Boston in 1924.) In late February 1923, Schooley
invited Conacher to referee two games at the Duquesne
Gardens to see if the Conacher magic worked with the
Pittsburgh fans. His experiment was a success. Schooley
also arranged for an exhibition tournament including
the Hamilton Tigers of the NHL, Aura Lee and the
Pittsburgh Yellow Jackets. Conacher was asked to play
with the senior amateur Pittsburgh team and
immediately caused a sensation by scoring eleven of his
team's twenty-three goals in the four games. And to
prime the public, Schooley wrote a highly
complimentary article outlining the Big Train's career in
Canada prior to the first game he refereed.

Schooley was determined to attract Conacher. There
was even the guarantee that his amateur status would be
protected. Conacher would be set up in business as an
insurance agent. Prospects were lined up for him,
prospects who were well-off. The commissions
generated by their life insurance purchases provided a
comfortable living for the new ice idol of Pittsburgh.
But perhaps the most important factor in Conacher's
decision was the opportunity to attend Bellefonte
Academy, a prep school in the Pittsburgh area where the
twenty-three-year-old could prepare to attend
university and play football.

In August 1923 Pittsburgh newspapers proudly
announced that "Canada's Premier Athlete" would
soon be arriving. But Toronto was less than thrilled
about its loss. One sportswriter lamented, "The success
of the United States of America in recently capturing the
Superman of Canada forms one of the Yankees' greatest
victories since the War of Independence." While
newspapers debated the pros and cons of such a move,
Conacher set about tying up one more loose end. In
September he eloped with Dorothy Kennedy, who was a

**PITTSBURGH'S YELLOW JACKETS**
UNITED STATES CHAMPIONS - 1923-1924

*Lionel Conacher (at left in middle row) and his Pittsburgh teammates*

noted athlete in her own right, an accomplished swimmer. Lionel, twenty-three, and Dorothy, seventeen, had not received her father's permission. For two years the unhappy father-in-law refused to speak to Lionel, but as Dorothy Conacher later said, "He wound up loving him."

The couple was married at the home of the Rev. J.A. Turnbull, and the reception was held at the home of Harris Ardiel. "The wedding," intoned the *World*, "aroused more interest and discussion than any other Toronto wedding in a long time." Prompted by the press coverage, one admirer sent the couple a cheque for $25, with instructions to buy a wedding gift. Conacher's

Hillcrest teammates bought him a travelling bag and a large floral horseshoe, which they draped over his shoulders. The couple decided that Dorothy should stay in Toronto to finish her course at the Margaret Eaton School of Expression. Her "Prince of Athletes" (named after the Prince of Wales, who was visiting Canada at the time) would start their married life in Pittsburgh without her.

*Dorothy Kennedy married Lionel Conacher in 1923.*

Conacher wasted no time in establishing his credentials. He soon became the star of the Bellefonte Academy football team, scoring four touchdowns in one game and "booting the ball a mile" in another. He then led Bellefonte to a championship 40-0 win over Carnegie Tech in the Tartan Bowl. In later years Carl Snavely, Lionel's football coach at Bellefonte, praised his former star player:

> Conacher, by the way, was probably the greatest athlete that I ever coached in football or any other form of athletics. . . .I don't believe I ever had a fullback who was a better runner in an open field, or who was a better punter, or who so fully possessed all the qualities of speed, skill, dexterity, aggressiveness, self-control, and the various attributes that are required for superiority in the American game of football. . . . In less than one season Conacher, who had never seen the American game played, became one of the outstanding prep school players of all time. He was far superior to a number of boys on the same team who later won All-American honors in several universities.

Conacher was outstanding as a football player, but he turned out to be a sensational Pittsburgh attraction as a hockey player. Selected to captain the Yellow Jackets (which was a totally Canadian team), he thrilled the fans with three goals in the first game.

When his team travelled to Boston to play, they were tabbed the "wonder team". Conacher was "Canada's Wonder Athlete". The Pittsburgh fans were ecstatic over their team's performance. A local sportswriter described the final game of the season as "the clatter of sticks, the clash of flying blades, a dazzling, all-pervading cloud of Gold, and overall, predominating the scene, the very air electric with the magic of his personality, Conacher, Lionel Conacher — Pittsburgh's mighty man of valor."

The amazing newcomer deserved all this

praise and more. He scored twenty-eight goals in twenty-nine games — all while playing part of Pittsburgh's "stonewall defence"! Conacher ended up topping the entire league with eighty-seven points! In rival Cleveland he was the "cat's pyjamas with all the fans", and in Pittsburgh reporters stretched higher and higher into hyperbole:

Weighted down by the responsibility and the knowledge that victory must come now or never, Conacher, like Hector of old, like Thor, the thundergod of Viking saga, bore up 'neath all to smite the enemy with a crashing blow.... Thrice did Lionel crack asunder that steely cordon Cleveland throws about her goal ... and thrice did 6000 fans rise up in roaring tribute to the man who in four brief months had become their idol.

The Pittsburgh fans' love affair with Conacher continued. A grateful public purchased him a new Hudson car when the Yellow Jackets became the United States hockey champions in 1923-24. The Conacher team repeated the victory in 1924-25. There seemed to be nothing that could stop the Big Train.

*Conacher with wedding gifts from the Hillcrest baseball team*

# Chapter 3 **Breaking Down**

In many ways the 1920s reflected the pattern of Lionel Conacher's career. The decade moved tentatively after World War I, hailed by some as the "war to end all wars". Then, feeling confident and secure, life began to rush ahead at a dizzying pace. Unbridled optimism coloured everything. The period was noted for dixieland swing, speakeasies, prohibition and life lived to the limits.

In sport, Queen's University was the most dominant Canadian football team of the early 1920s, winning three consecutive Grey Cup titles. Baseball's New York Yankees, with the "Sultan of Swat" Babe Ruth and the "Iron Man" Lou Gehrig, were idols of an adoring public. The Golden Age of Sport was in full bloom. As the decade unfolded, Canada steadily moved away from the traditional British influences and more towards those of the United States. In 1924 the National Hockey League expanded to its first American city, Boston. At the same time Montreal established its second NHL team, the Maroons, a club identified with the city's English minority. Further NHL expansion took place in 1925, when the Hamilton Tigers franchise was moved to the United States and became the New York Americans. The Hamilton team had finished on top of the NHL in the spring of 1925. However, the players chose to strike for an extra $200 per man for the championship series. The NHL balked, suspended Hamilton and sold its franchise to New York, where the new Madison Square Garden eagerly awaited its team, the Americans. At the same time, the announcement was made that Pittsburgh would be awarded an NHL franchise.

Lionel Conacher was faced with a dilemma. In 1923 and 1924 he had been able to lead the Yellow Jackets to the amateur national title. He had also been prominent in football at Bellefonte and Duquesne University during those two years. To commit himself openly to professional sport meant that football was out of the question, since it was still only an amateur sport. It also meant that his formal education would come to an end. Although Lionel had received earlier professional hockey offers, it was not until 1925 that his situation tempted him to accept a contract. He was now a married man who was moving past his peak athletic years. Hockey was not his best sport, but it offered the greatest opportunity for a lengthy career in an established league.

After much thought, Lionel Conacher signed his first professional contract with the new Pittsburgh NHL entry on November 11, 1925. Fans and management were enthusiastic and optimistic. After all, the entire Yellow Jacket team had "turned pro". Throughout the discussions leading up to the awarding of the franchise, the signing of players and the courting of Lionel Conacher, it was suggested that the player-manager of the new franchise, the Pirates, might be Conacher himself. But it was not to be.

*During a practice session Conacher demonstrates his famous "travelling netminder" pose.*

The post of player-manager was awarded to Odie Cleghorn, an eight-year veteran with the Montreal Canadiens. Conacher was disappointed to lose the job as manager, but he tried to forget about it and concentrate on his game. The Pirates won their first game against Boston, with Conacher scoring the first goal for the new franchise. For six weeks Conacher's play attracted rave notices in the press. Cleghorn's tactics, however, were constantly questioned. Instead of using two lines and leaving them on the ice for longer periods of time, he pioneered the use of three lines and short shifts. This new game plan — and the failure to award Conacher the manager's post — caused considerable trouble on the team. The situation finally erupted into the open, and by the end of the season it was predicted that Cleghorn would not be with Pittsburgh much longer.

In addition to talk about the Pirates hockey club, the 1925-26 sports news included the announcement in January 1926 that the Big Train had signed to play professional baseball with the Toronto Maple Leafs, a team in the International League. The club was ecstatic. Even though Conacher had not played baseball for three years, the club owners were convinced that he still had tremendous gate appeal. Conacher, for his part, wrote into his contract that he could not be sold or traded during the season. Both parties seemed to benefit from the arrangement. Although Conacher did not play much, fans were attracted to the park, and the Leafs won the International League championship as well as the Little World Series. In the course of the summer Conacher was compared favourably by one American sportswriter to Frankie Frisch and George Sisler, two of the greatest diamond men of all time.

That fall Conacher returned to Pittsburgh, but it was obvious that the problems on his hockey team had not been solved. Three more teams, New York, Chicago and Detroit, had entered the NHL. Conacher was traded to the New York Americans in December 1926. The move revitalized him. Newsy Lalonde was the coach and Billy Burch was a star performer. The rest of the Americans were considered the playboys of the NHL. They were much more press-conscious than were the Rangers, New York's other pro hockey team. In their opening game of

*One of many sports cartoons celebrating Conacher's wide range of athletic skills*

the 1925 season, the first professional game played in New York, the Montreal Canadiens provided the opposition. The contest was described as "ballyhoo at its best". Some said it took half an hour to enter the new Madison Square Garden. The combined forces of the Governor General's band and the West Point band inspired players and spectators.

Lionel was soon the toast of New York, enjoying the change in scenery and the lavish attention paid to the Americans. Conacher was a thinking hockey player. His mind was able to "figure out angles at which it was impossible for even a fast-breaking forward to break clear on the net." In this way he could play down his awkward skating and keep his opponents between him and the boards. He soon became famous for his "travelling netminder" style of defensive play. He would become a second goalkeeper, effortlessly dropping to one knee and smothering shots. Before long the New York papers were describing his play as brilliant.

Publicity followed Conacher everywhere, and New York's discovery of his past athletic skills led to Conacher's return to football. For two years, 1927 and 1928, he worked as an assistant coach at Rutgers University in nearby New Jersey. He still showed outstanding ability in the sport that had always been his first love. Although it was four years since he had last played, he often joined the second string in practice games against the varsity. Twice he carried the ball seventy-five yards past the stunned first team.

There was a danger that the rapid expansion of the National Hockey League in the late 1920s might spread the hockey talent too thin. But such was not the case. The newly acquired franchises were soon stocked with established players from the Western Canada Hockey League, a professional circuit that was having financial difficulties. It was "go East, young man", as players such as Frank Boucher, Bill and Bun Cook, Ebbie Goodfellow and Frank Frederickson formed the core of the new NHL teams.

In the midst of these quality players it was soon apparent that Conacher's game was off. Perhaps it was because he had fallen in with the undisciplined New York Americans. Perhaps there were too many distractions. Whatever the reasons, Lionel Conacher was definitely undergoing his own October 24, 1929 — Black Thursday. He had started drinking heavily and often. His brother Charlie remarked that Lionel seemed "bent on a literal interpretation of the soft drink slogan 'Drink Canada Dry!'" New York traded him to the Montreal Maroons in time for the 1930 season. The Conacher name still carried a punch, but Lionel Conacher, an overly confident thirty-year-old by this time, was not as conscious as others that his play was lacking. In effect, he was an alcoholic fooling himself. The Maroons decided to put him on waivers. It seemed that the Big Train was about to be derailed.

# Refuelling Chapter 4

The Great Depression of the 1930s plunged Canada —
and much of the Western world — into poverty and
despondency. The optimism and promise of the 1920s
were now only a memory. With each passing day the
paralyzing Depression seemed to tighten its grip on the
nation. Unemployment, soup lines, hobo jungles, prairie
droughts — all these brought home the reality of a
broken-down economy and a desperate population. The
bright hopes of the early decades of the twentieth
century seemed dim and long ago. The Depression years
proved to be a test of the nation's will to rise again and
reassert its strengths and determination.

So too with Lionel Conacher. If he were to reach his
former heights, he would have to summon up all the will

*During the Depression
thousands of unemployed people
travelled back and forth across
Canada on boxcars, stopping in
various towns to look for work.
What are some of the economic
factors that lead to a depression?
What are some of the problems
in Canada's economy today?*

# RALLY FOLLOWS PANICKY STOCK SELLING

## TERRIFIC SELLING WAVE ENDS: N.Y. STOCKS REBOUND

### Strenuous Efforts of Great Banks Turn Stampede of Frantic Sellers During Record Day on Wall Street

### Prices Crash to New Depths On All Marts When Holders Dump Big Blocks into Pits

### Canadian Securities Quite Sound, Dominion Government Officials Say

### Utter Collapse in Stock Market Narrowly Averted

### 25 Billion Dollars in Quoted Values Wiped Out in Tremendous Market Crash Which Puts Over Five Hundred Issues at New Low Levels

*Headlines in* The Ottawa Evening Citizen, The Winnipeg Evening Tribune *and* The Globe *in Toronto on the eve of the great stock market crash of 1929. Why did the market crash?*

power he possessed. By 1930 he was said to be drinking two bottles of hard liquor each day. In some ways he was again the twelve-year-old boy begging his father to give him the chance to drive the team of horses. To pull himself out of alcoholism, he had to believe "I can do it, I can do it!"

As a boy Lionel had felt that he wanted to help out at home. He had relished the chance to contribute to the welfare of his family. The family proved important to Lionel at an older age too. Sport had become the way he helped his family rise from the poverty he had known as a youngster. In some ways the family had come to depend on him. Even after Lionel was married, he made regular visits to his parents' house, leaving money in different places, enjoying what he was to call the "hunt". After Charlie Conacher joined Toronto's NHL team, the Maple Leafs, the two brothers organized the hunt together, both delighted that they were able to help the family live an easier life.

When Charlie signed his first contract with Toronto in 1929, Lionel was there acting as his adviser. Lionel had urged Charlie to sign with the Leafs, even though he was coaching with the New York Americans at the time. He figured that it would be better for a kid of nineteen to break into the professionals in his home town. The New York team was "a pretty free-wheeling crew off the ice".

Charlie had always listened eagerly to Lionel, who was nine years older. From the start the older brother had suggested that weak-skating Charlie should keep practising to improve his skill. Lionel continually stressed that hockey could provide the escape from poverty. Knowing full well the appeal that the name Conacher had in Toronto, he was determined that teams would pay for it.

Charlie signed a two-year contract for $20 000, with an advance payment of $5000. To underscore the fact that this was a lot of money, Depression or not, Conn Smythe, owner of the Maple Leafs, paid the bonus with five thousand one-dollar bills. Charlie was so excited that he immediately bought a yellow Buick coupe with a rumble seat, picked up some sandwiches and drove home to show the family. Everyone piled into the car and headed out for a picnic. As Lionel had done before him, Charlie organized races for the younger members of the family, especially the twins, Roy and Bert, Kay and Nora. It really didn't matter who won. The dollar prize was always shared equally.

By 1930, however, it appeared that Lionel's ability to contribute to the family income was in danger. When the Maroons put him on waivers, Lionel suddenly realized that his career was finished unless he could find the discipline of his younger, hungrier years. In November 1930 Conacher's need to reform himself became even more urgent. In Toronto's Wellesley Hospital, on November 25, a daughter, Constance, was born to Dorothy and Lionel. The birth seemed to spark Conacher's spirit and will power. He promised his wife "Dot" that from then on "things would be different." Rather than move to Montreal from New York, Lionel decided to live in Toronto, where they could be close to both families. Their new home at 55 Teddington Avenue would become the centre of his life.

And things were different, but not before more misfortune. Within the space of eight months Conacher

*Charlie Conacher*

had stopped drinking completely, but contracted pneumonia. It was going to take all his strength and determination to get back on the track. First the pneumonia had to be overcome. Then there was the constant craving for alcohol. It took tremendous will power to resist the daily torment, but Conacher held on. As if that wasn't enough, he was hospitalized and operated on to remove a "painful growth".

These terrible months tested every ounce of strength and single-mindedness in Lionel Conacher. Over and over again he muttered his boyhood promise, "I can do it, I can do it." The craving for drink was so intense that he consumed soft drinks and chocolate to remove the temptation. During the long struggle Lionel knew he had to fill his days with activity to keep him away from alcohol. He became a dedicated tea drinker — he drank pots of tea daily — and a pipe smoker for the rest of his life. Golf helped him occupy his time. When he was not practising or playing hockey, he would play thirty-six, even forty-five, holes of golf at a public course in Montreal or Toronto.

Often he would attend movies by himself during the day or night. The strain on his nervous system was so great that he was able to sit still for only part of each movie. He would often make a note of the length of the movie and the time he had to leave. He would then return another day to see the remainder. Once he was well enough to skate and practise, he drove himself hard to build up his skill and confidence. This difficult year was later described by Conacher himself:

It was in 1930 that I experienced my hardest battle as an athlete . . . an unwanted veteran with the Maroons, who were trying unsuccessfully to waive me out of the league. I promptly decided to quit drinking, and it was the training of many gruelling years in sport — making the old will power say "Uncle" — that stood me in good stead. . . it was a tough fight, I'm telling you, getting out of the broken-down, has-been rut, and none realize the job it was better than myself.

Lionel's determination and improved play paid off. The Maroons, impressed by his revitalized game, decided to take their chances with Conacher for another season. Lionel rose to the challenge and ended up being selected by his teammates as the most valuable Maroon player for the 1931-32 season. He was on his way to a full recovery.

Strange as it may seem, professional sport flourished

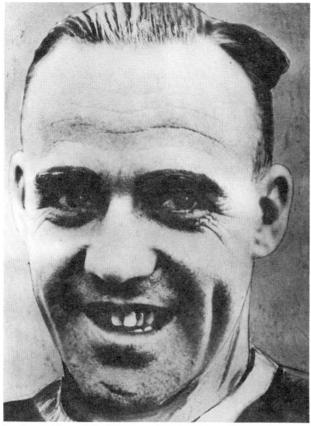

*Frank "King" Clancy, one of the most popular figures in the history of the Toronto Maple Leafs, was paid $35 000 to join the Leafs in 1930. Why do you think sport was so popular during the Depression?*

in the midst of the Depression. For one thing, the media — newspapers and the relatively new radio — generated immense publicity. When a player "turned professional", the press coverage did much to lay the groundwork for the eventual acceptance of professional sport. At a time when it was almost impossible to find any work, there was a certain mystique surrounding the large salaries being paid to hockey players. Today we can only imagine the amazement people felt when they learned that the Leafs paid Ottawa $35 000 *plus* two players for Frank "King" Clancy. Because of its scarcity, money meant instant status. Clancy — and by extension the Maple Leaf hockey players, the NHL and all professional athletes — bathed in the public recognition. Frank Selke, in his memoirs, *Behind the Cheering*, suggested that the opening of Maple Leaf Gardens in the depths of the Depression was "the single most important factor in giving the game its new status."

There can be no doubt about the influence radio had in the 1930s on the acceptance of sport in general and professional sport and hockey in particular. During one Saturday night broadcast, sports commentator Foster Hewitt announced that for ten cents listeners could order a special issue of the Maple Leafs program highlighting the new building plans. By Monday three huge mailbags, containing ninety thousand requests, were delivered to the Maple Leafs office. Despite all the hardships, spectator sport was booming. To take advantage of the obvious public interest, the Toronto *Globe* announced that as of January 20, 1933, sports news would be given much more prominence. The first page of the second section would headline the expanded coverage, which was to include illustrations and a daily sports cartoon.

The success of professional hockey, the influence of press and radio and the new climate for sport led to renewed interest in lacrosse. Ever since 1867 the myth has been kept alive that lacrosse is Canada's national game by virtue of government legislation. A Montreal

*The 1869 lacrosse champions of Canada were players from the Caughnawaga Indian Reserve. For centuries native people in North America played lacrosse both as a game and as part of religious rituals. Who are the great lacrosse players today?*

dentist, Dr. George Beers, known as the "father of Canadian lacrosse", was probably responsible for the beginnings of the myth. He wrote a regular newspaper column entitled "The National Game". When the National Lacrosse Association was formed in 1867 and reported in Beer's column, the myth was born and has continued to this day. Some people have called lacrosse the "national game" because of the uniqueness of this North American sport and because of the high level it reached in Canada, first among the Indians who started the game and later among other athletes. Prior to 1931 lacrosse was a field game, closely resembling the original sport played among the native people. As baseball and football increased in spectator appeal, lacrosse suffered. In 1931, however, the game was changed so that it could be played indoors, usually on the unfrozen surface of a hockey rink. Rinks and players were available, and the public was ready to give lacrosse a chance.

A four-team professional indoor lacrosse league was formed in 1931 with two teams representing Montreal (the Canadiens and Maroons) and one team each from Cornwall and Toronto. Widespread publicity led up to the opening game between the Maroons and the Leafs. Primo Carnera, the first non-American to hold the world heavyweight title since Canada's Tommy Burns, was in Toronto for a boxing match and officiated at the opening face-off ceremony. The Maroons lineup read like a Who's Who of well-known athletes: Hooley Smith, Nels Stewart, Ted Reeve, Dunc Munro and, of course, Lionel Conacher. All these athletes welcomed the chance to turn professional in a new sport.

The situation was ideal for the Big Train. The challenge of a brand new professional league revitalized him. Ever since he had become a professional athlete, he had been forced to give up his many other sporting activities. Now it was like old times! He threw himself into the new lacrosse league with all his energy. Much to the delight of the fans and the promoters, Lionel Conacher once again proved to be a powerhouse. He led the Maroons to the championship and won the scoring title with 107 points. His nearest competitor had only fifty-six.

# Chapter 5 **Whistle Stops**

While the country sank deeper into the depths of a depression, Lionel Conacher rose to the challenge of his dramatic return to prominence. Perhaps, too, he was even more aware of the relatively insecure life of the professional athlete. He had come within a whisker of losing all that he had worked so hard for. He had almost forgotten that determination and constant effort had been his biggest assets in rising from poverty. At best, Conacher thought he might have three or four years left to make the most of his athletic talent. And at the same time Conacher's family was expanding. His second daughter, Diane, was born in January 1932.

A third consideration was the National Hockey League's ruling in 1933 that the total salary budget for any one team could not exceed $70 000. The highest individual salary was limited to $10 000 (at least over the table, suggested one joker). In any event, clubs were pressing to lower salaries in the Depression years. Involvement in other professional sports would not only add to Conacher's income, it would also give him an edge in his contract negotiations with the Maroons. And so, Lionel Conacher decided to embark on a professional wrestling career.

Conacher had not wrestled since 1916, when he was lightweight champion of Ontario. But he was big, strong and extremely well known. Radio coverage of his hockey and lacrosse exploits had brought Conacher's name to rural areas and small towns. His wrestling matches would also be broadcast. On November 2, 1931, it was announced that Lionel Conacher had signed a three-year contract with Toronto promoter, Ivan Mickailoff. Conacher was to receive $7000 the first year, $10 000 the second and $15 000 the third. However the Maroons, worried that a wrestling injury might ruin Conacher's hockey season, paid Mickailoff to keep Conacher out of wrestling matches until the end of the hockey season.

Rather than play lacrosse during the summer of 1932, Conacher wrestled. Every match generated publicity, and big crowds turned out to see the famous athlete. His first match, against Karl Pospeshil, was broadcast by two Toronto radio stations. Pre-match publicity highlighted Conacher's rugged approach to sport.                    "Flying tackles, speed, strength plus unlimit- ed courage" thrilled the 5500 spectators who had paid to see Conacher's first venture into this new combination of sport and entertainment. Everywhere Lionel Conacher, the Big Train, went — London, Windsor, Montreal — the fans adored him. Conacher won all twenty-six matches dur- ing the summer of 1932. But perhaps more important to his career and to sport in general, he made a vivid impression on many who had previously been unable to see a first-class professional athlete in action. Many of his matches ended with a standing ovation as he left the ring.

During the 1932-33 hockey season, the Conacher legend continued to grow. He was named to the NHL All-Star team. His hockey ability seemed to flourish with each new off-season activity he added to his schedule. The public seemed starved for sport. Newspapers, the radio and the public buzzed with excitement when Conacher announced that he would form Canada's first professional football team in 1933. Conacher had turned down an opportunity to coach the Montreal Winged Wheelers in 1931, when the forward pass was intro- duced in eastern Canada. It was the first year that the forward pass was used in all senior leagues across Canada as well as the Grey Cup game. In effect, the new forward pass changed Canadian football from its pre- dominantly running character to a passing game, as in the United States. As much as Conacher would have wanted, his professional sports activities kept him from playing for the amateur Winged Wheelers. However, because of his coaching experience with Rutgers Univer- sity, he was asked to coach the Montreal team. Conacher declined. He had other plans.

In 1933 Conacher signed a contract with a food company, Crosse and Blackwell, to organize and coach a

*Conacher kicking off for the Crosse and Blackwell Chefs*

professional team, the Chefs. The Toronto team would compete with American teams, and Conacher immediately began recruiting professional athletes with a football background for the Thanksgiving Day opening of the new club's season. Charlie Conacher joined his brother, who was still remembered as "the greatest rugby player of all time".

Thirteen thousand spectators turned out to witness the first game with Rochester. Although the Toronto team lost the exhibition 18-15, those who came to see Conacher were not disappointed:

> . . .never in his career did he give such a sterling performance. It was remarkable the way he weaved his way through broken and battled fields for long gains. "Conny" scored the first touchdown of the game when he sprinted around the end for 20 yards, and later on he raced 75 yards for another major count. Then in the dying moments of the struggle he took a pass from Charlie Conacher, raced to the 30-yard line and passed to "Duke" McCurry who went the rest of the way.

*Lionel Conacher, defence star for the Chicago Black Hawks. With so many high-calibre hockey teams across Canada, why were most NHL franchises established in American cities during the 1920s and 1930s?*

The team's second game, with Buffalo, was an 18-0 victory for Toronto. The *Globe* singled out the performance of Lionel Conacher. Once again the Big Train was "the whole show, giving further proof that he must be considered as the greatest grid performer of the decade." This despite the fact that Conacher had not played serious football for nine years.

The exciting experiment in football continued that season, while Lionel Conacher made preparations to join his fourth team in the National Hockey League, the Chicago Black Hawks. That year, 1933-34, the amazing Conacher led the Black Hawks to their first Stanley Cup and was selected to the All-Star team. Conacher seemed almost superhuman, and the legend of "Canada's greatest athlete" flourished more than ever before.

But the Conacher mythology would never have been complete without Conn Smythe, owner of the Toronto Maple Leafs and a celebrity in his own right. As coach of the Varsity Grads, winners of the Allan Cup in 1923-24 and of the Olympics in 1924, Smythe had made quite a reputation as a hockey man. As an expert judge of talent, he was paid $10 000 by the New York Rangers, a new NHL franchise in 1926, to find and sign players. Smythe recruited the likes of Bill and Bun Cook, Ching Johnson, Taffy Abel and Frank Boucher. However, he had also been offered the services of Babe Dye from the Toronto St. Patricks. Dye was a veteran "name" player, but Smythe was convinced that Dye did not suit the style of the team he was building. When Smythe refused to sign Dye, an action that angered Ranger president John Hammond, Smythe was told that he was through and given $7500 as a settlement.

For the Rangers' opening game under new coach Lester Patrick, Smythe journeyed to New York to watch the collection he had assembled. When the Rangers put on a sparkling display in defeating the Montreal Maroons 1-0, Madison Square Garden boxing promoter Tex Rickard suggested that Smythe should be "vice-president in charge of hockey at the Garden". The fiery Smythe shot back that he wouldn't take such a job from

Conn Smythe owned the Maple Leafs hockey club from 1927 to 1961 and led his team to seven Stanley Cups. In addition to his fame in hockey and thoroughbred racing circles, Smythe was known for his charitable work with the deaf and with crippled children.

a group who didn't know how to treat people and still owed him $2500. When the president of Madison Square Garden heard the story, he ordered a cheque for $2500 to be paid to Smythe, who took a train to Montreal, where he bet the entire amount on a University of Toronto-McGill football game. The gamble paid off, and Smythe took all his winnings and bet on the Toronto St. Pats to beat the Ottawa Senators in an NHL game. Again he won. Suddenly armed with a substantial amount of money, Smythe formed a partnership with mining millionaire J.P. Bickell and broker Peter Campbell to buy the Toronto St. Pats — later renamed the Maple Leafs.

As much as anyone in Canada, Smythe was responsible for and benefited from the increased publicity for sport during the late 1920s and 1930s. He was quick to recognize the impact that the Big Train had on the Toronto public. When he signed Charlie to the Maple Leafs in 1929, Smythe realized that the very name Conacher would attract customers. Smythe drew many of his players from the Toronto area and was promoting the local flavour of the Maple Leafs. He was eager to show that with some encouragement from the public they could compare favourably with any of the teams in the NHL who drew talent from across Canada. The Maple Leaf program advertising the first game between Charlie Conacher and his brother Lionel (then playing for New York) featured a full-page appeal:

Next Tuesday evening Lionel Conacher and his New York Americans will be here to tackle the Leafs. Young Charlie is anxious to hold up his end against his famous brother, and we are doing all in our power to have you help out en masse to help the "sniping Duke" do the trick. Being only a kid, Charlie is at the impressionable age when concerted cheering can help him do the impossible. New York writers think that he is a sensation. Come out and help us convince the Big Train the praise is merited.

Charlie Conacher was also an impressive athlete. He proved to be an outstanding player in the NHL as part of the Leafs' famous "Kid Line". Promoters in all the NHL cities tried to create the impression that the Big Train and his brother, the Human Express, were heading for a collision. Lionel's style of play lent itself to such publicity, particularly when the press reminded people of his wrestling, lacrosse and football skills. His towering figure stood even taller on skates, and his preference for physical contact meant that he had developed a reputation as a "tough" athlete. He once told how "in 1922 a colossal man came roaring from the stands 'to tear me to bits.' He went to the hospital and I had to leave town on the q.t."

The Big Train constantly impressed spectators, opponents and reporters with the raw physical power of his game. Whether it was flying tackles in wrestling; rink-length, speed-gathering rushes in hockey; battering ram and explosive running in football; or cradling the lacrosse ball against his body while steaming towards the opponents' goal area — all these reinforced the image of Conacher's sheer physical dominance. With so much publicity emphasizing Conacher's strength and courage, few fans would have believed the fear that gripped the Big Train each time he made his semi-annual visit to the dentist. The prospect of having his teeth drilled terrified the big, brave superstar. But in the press Conacher was always larger than such day-to-day concerns.

*This famous picture now hangs in Canada's Sports Hall of Fame*

In anticipation of Lionel's first game at Maple Leaf Gardens in the 1933-34 season, Smythe arranged for the Toronto newspapers to build up the confrontation between the two local favourites. A newspaper picture, almost half-page in size, showed Charlie Conacher skating in front of a fast-moving steam engine racing in the same direction as a sign pointing to the NHL championship. A picture of Lionel over a caption,

"The Big Train", was placed at the front of the hurtling express. Charlie was saying, "So long Lion'l. I can't wait for you." The heading above the advertisement declared: "Brotherly Love will Cease To-night at Maple Leaf Gardens When the Chicago Black Hawks and Leafs Clash."

Lionel and Charlie appeared only too willing to oblige those who were looking for a family feud. That evening the two were given penalties for high sticking. Charlie Conacher later explained:

As we neared the penalty box, Lionel stuck his face against my chin and started talking animatedly, waving his arms and scowling. I snarled back at him, bobbing my head to emphasize my annoyance. 'I didn't get around to the house today' is what Lionel actually said to me. 'Are Mom and Dad okay?' 'Sure they're fine' is what I was telling him, 'but they wondered why you didn't come home.' As we were leaving the penalty box after serving our two minutes, Lionel grabbed my sweater to hold me back. I gestured threateningly at him and the two of us skated to our positions, still scowling.

The crowd thoroughly enjoyed the "confrontation".

In spite of Lionel Conacher's great reputation and his being from Toronto, he was usually greeted in Maple Leaf Gardens with a chorus of boos. They were "respectful" boos, the type a great athlete receives when he comes up against the local favourites. Other famous hockey players were to go through this razzing as well — Richard, Howe, Orr and Esposito. However, the booing bothered Conacher so much that he publicly declared that under no circumstances would he ever play NHL hockey with Toronto. This possibility was suggested more than once because Charlie was with the Leafs.

If there was any doubt about the loyalty of the Toronto hockey fans, there was certainly none in other areas. Chicago followers were so delighted when Conacher and the Black Hawks won the Stanley Cup, they gave the club a ten-minute standing ovation. It was Chicago's and Conacher's first Stanley Cup and signalled a new flurry of involvement by the man who was described as "Canada's premier all-round athlete". Conacher had told a reporter for the New York *Sun* that athletes should take part in sport throughout the year and keep every muscle in the body in active working condition. The paper accepted that as sound advice, but wondered how many athletes were capable of putting it

*Conacher in the uniform of his second professional football team, the Wrigley Aromints*

into practice. "It must be borne in mind," the *Sun* wrote of Conacher, "that he is the greatest all round athlete developed in Canada and has a claim to being the greatest developed anywhere, including these United States, that produced Jim Thorpe."

Conacher played professional football again in 1934, this time under the sponsorship of the Wrigley Gum Company. Known as the Aromints, the club featured Lionel and Charlie and a mixture of Canadian and American rules. The "Men of Conacher" continued to make sports news during 1934, and the newspapers seemed to be vying with each other for news about the "Big Train of Canadian Sport". The sports editor of the *Globe*, Mike Rodden, Lionel's former coach with the Argonauts, eagerly followed the Aromints and provided many inside stories for *Globe* readers. But the greatest publicity was reserved for the announcement by the Toronto *Telegram* that Lionel Conacher was to write a daily column on football during the coming football season. When J.P. Fitzgerald, the *Telegram's* sports editor, announced the Conacher series, he reported that the *Telegram* wanted to improve the quality of young, upcoming football players. Sponsored by the *Telegram*, Conacher would visit local high schools to give tips on the game and then follow up the visit with an article in the paper.

Conacher was delighted with the new job. He claimed that it was his "greatest thrill" and that his "life ambition was to write sport and next to that . . . to write about football." Each day, *Telegram* readers were greeted with a picture of Conacher, an article highlighting a Toronto high school and a discussion of an area of football — all under the byline, "Lionel Conacher, Canada's Greatest Athlete". The night prior to his first article a quarter-page picture of Conacher in football togs advertised the series, dubbing him "The Greatest Rugby Player of All Time". The series was a huge success and continued until Conacher was forced to leave in October for training camp in Winnipeg with the Montreal Maroons. It appears that the Maroons soon realized how foolish they had been to send Conacher to Chicago. They persuaded the Canadiens to trade for Conacher and then made arrangements to obtain him for the Maroons.

*The public always seemed eager for stories and pictures of Lionel Conacher. This 1934 cartoon in the sports section of the The Globe was created by Charles "Chuck" Templeton, now a well-known author.*

Before his departure, however, the Toronto public once again had the opportunity to watch the versatile athlete in still another sport. It was announced that Lionel would be among a group of NHL All-Stars competing with the Maple Leafs baseball team in a hospital benefit game. The largest crowd of the season, some two thousand, showed up to watch "Big Train Lionel Conacher, [who] was of course the gent who drew the keenest scrutiny of the occasion, reaching base four times while collecting three hits."

In 1932 a *Maclean's* writer noted that the public had learned that Conacher's "presence in the midst of a sporting fray has always been an assurance of thrills and excitement." Especially in the 1930s, in the depths of the Depression, Lionel Conacher stood out as a light in the gloom of a world not only broken-down but heading once again towards the horrors of war. Perhaps the times were such that there was a need for heroes and legends, a need to forget the day-to-day cares of trying to struggle along and eke out a living. Ethiopia, Manchuria, the Rhineland were all far away. Sport was here, and all that "News of the World" wasn't. It was said that "the era of the Thirties was born in disaster, lived in turmoil and expired in a whimper." But that description didn't fit sport and certainly didn't fit Lionel Conacher.

The 1934-35 hockey season proved to be one of Lionel's best. Once again he led his team, this time the Montreal Maroons, to a Stanley Cup victory over the Leafs. Extensive newspaper coverage of the series included a multitude of photographs featuring Conacher. Apparently the public could not get enough. Lionel and Charlie were granted permission by the City of Toronto to purchase land at the corner of Yonge and Davenport in order to build a service station. The grand opening in the summer of 1935 resulted in near chaos:

For more than two hours, cars in a steady line were driven into the station. Hundreds of men and boys attended, and before the evening closed, the Conachers, in spite of their winter training, had their arms stiffened in "writer's cramp" from slinging down their autographs.

Perhaps because of his growing family responsibilities — Lionel Jr. was born in 1936 — Lionel Conacher decided to end his athletic career in the NHL in the spring of 1937. It was a difficult year for the Montreal public. Within one month, two of their idols were gone. In March Howie Morenz of the Canadiens suffered a heart attack and died. During his twelve years with the Canadiens he had been the idol of thousands and a model for youth to emulate:

Morenz was far more than a Canadian hero. To youngsters all over Canada he was to hockey what Babe Ruth was to baseball and Jack Dempsey to boxing — a fairy tale figure who could do things no one else could do and against greater odds. When Morenz duped a defenceman, it was David slaying Goliath.

*An advertising calendar from the Conachers' service station in Toronto. What kinds of businesses are professional athletes involved in in Canada today?*

Then in April Lionel Conacher retired from hockey. Whether it was a coincidence or not, the Maroon franchise was to last only one year longer before the team withdrew from the NHL. But the Big Train wasn't about to end his career completely. He would soon be rolling along again, this time on a different track.

# New Tracks Chapter 6

For most athletes who have spent their careers in the limelight, fawned upon by an adoring public, retirement can be a shattering experience. Day by day it becomes more and more evident that the spotlight of fame is shifting. No longer is he or she wanted for interviews. Now no one asks for opinions on game strategy, new players, coaching changes or a host of other topics that make the news. Some other idol has replaced the older athlete in the public eye, usually with no noticeable disruption. But Lionel Conacher was not like most people. His whole life had hinged upon initiative and determination. He had risen to great heights because of these outstanding qualities of his character — but not without costs.

Prior to his NHL retirement, Conacher wrote an article in the September 1, 1936, issue of *Maclean's*, recounting the cost involved in establishing his career. He gave a long list of injuries: nose broken eight times (so often that many suggested it be put on a hinge); a broken arm and leg; several broken bones in his hands; ten cracked ribs; skate gashes across the jugular vein requiring sixteen stitches ("which had me a matter of inches away from eternity"); a cut on the thigh ("which resulted in gangrene and a red-hot bout with the Grim Reaper"); two knee cartilage operations; 650 stitches (five hundred in his face and head area) plus "innumerable routine injuries classed 'minor', which include sundry sprains, pulled ligaments, twisted muscles, black eyes, bumps, aches, bruises, etc." All of which led Conacher to describe his appearance as less than aristocratic.

There were psychological costs too, especially the effort required to force "the old will power to make the body say 'Uncle' when said body is howling for an easy chair, unrestricted diet and the odd gay party, instead of constantly wincing under the lash of the Big Time's rigorous training rules." Conacher ate only one meal per day with an apple or piece of chocolate to supplement it. He was seldom able to fall asleep immediately; night

*Do you think professional athletes deserve the high salaries they are paid in sports such as football, hockey and baseball?*

after night his pent-up nerves kept him wide awake until three in the morning. As to whether the life of an athlete was carefree, Conacher suggested that one should spend some time with a losing team or be in a slump, wondering where the axe will fall next. While many fans consider travel glamorous and exciting, the Big Train suggested that the fans should "toss in a few rugged, bumping, bruising hockey games with those train rides before and after, if you want to get a true picture of the [athlete's] 'soft life'."

Conacher's reputation for being a tough athlete meant that he always had to watch out for "people who seek glory by downing athletes with such reputations." Though he dreaded the time when he had to quit sport ("There constantly lurks in my mind a dread that I've reached the point where I'll be unable to repeat the things I've done in the past"), Conacher insisted that he would gladly do it all again the same way: "It cost me plenty but I've reaped plenty of dividends in thrills, happiness and financial security. A career in the Big Time is worthwhile because to make a success of it, you must build your body, think clearly and lead a regular life."

*Dorothy and Lionel Conacher and their five children. What happened to other famous Canadian athletes, such as Ned Hanlan, Tom Longboat and Maurice Richard, when they retired from professional sport?*

Lionel Conacher played his last professional hockey game on April 23, 1937, at the age of thirty-seven. But retirement did little to slow down his busy lifestyle. Having been a member of the Maroons, a team owned by stockbrokers, who often gave him investment tips, Conacher bought into a brokerage firm in Toronto. The earnings of his past athletic career were soundly invested, thanks to the friendship and advice of Harry Seguin of the Toronto Stock Exchange and Brian Newkirk, a businessman and promoter. During his athletic career Conacher met many influential people, including important entrepreneurs and politicians. Lionel seemed to have a strong personality that attracted people to him. Not the least of these was Mitchell Hepburn, Liberal candidate for premier of Ontario in the upcoming 1937 provincial election. Hepburn encouraged Conacher to use his public appeal to secure the Liberal nomination for the Bracondale riding, which included Lionel's childhood home.

His wide-ranging popularity as an athlete stood Conacher in good stead, and he won the nomination. In his acceptance speech Conacher spoke of his wish to develop a sports program for the youth of Ontario. He admitted that he was a "green amateur" in politics but stressed his ability to understand the problems of the poor in the riding. These problems, Conacher reasoned, were similar to the ones his family had known in the early 1900s.

The novice politician attacked his election campaign with the same dogged determination he had demonstrated as an athlete. At the same time he continued to appear in charity benefit games as a player, referee or umpire. Not being a gifted speaker, Conacher used his well-known name on posters, on radio program announcements and on advertisements for public picnics, which he hosted for his potential constituents. Conacher knew it would be an uphill fight because Bracondale was traditionally a Conservative stronghold. He promised only that, since he knew what was needed in the riding, he would "go after it for the residents of the district. . . . I'll certainly be working for them in the legislature." By a slim margin of thirty-seven votes Lionel Conacher, the Big Train, became Lionel Conacher MPP. His opponent, Russell Nesbitt, was awarded a

**Don't Fail to Vote!**

No man can be considered Canada's greatest all-round athlete and not be capable of tackling Youth and other problems and ably assisting in their proper solution. Lionel Conacher appeals to you for an opportunity to help YOU and YOUTH.

**Vote for and Elect**

# LIONEL CONACHER

LIBERAL   **BRACONDALE**   CANDIDATE

*A Conacher campaign poster in 1937. Why are people likely to vote for a famous person when he or she runs for political office? What qualities that make a good athlete would also make a good politician?*

recount, but the Conservative candidate still fell short and somewhat bitterly accepted defeat.

As soon as he was elected, Conacher the politician set off energetically on visits throughout Ontario. He was with Acting Premier Nixon at the Huntsville Carnival; he represented Premier Hepburn at a St. Thomas baseball banquet; he bailed out a wrestling benefit in Ottawa, which Jack Dempsey was supposed to referee. When Dempsey was forced to withdraw because of illness, Conacher assured the success of the charity match, which was in support of a local Christmas fund. Premier Hepburn and Lionel Conacher became very close friends and often travelled together on business, hunting and vacation trips. At all these affairs Conacher would be flooded with autograph requests while the local stars were all but ignored.

But politics was more than sport. One of the first things the newly elected MPP did was to set up an office over his service station to handle visits from his constituents. Under the direction of his sister Nora, the office welcomed a steady flow of people looking for solutions to their problems. More often than not, solutions were found — and Conacher never sought publicity for his actions. Funeral expenses were provided for a constituent whose husband died; fuel bills were paid for the poor; immigration problems were sorted out. From his headquarters in 1937 Conacher sent proposals to the premier to make a camp in Orillia available to youngsters from all across the province and to stop the financial exploitation of young boxers by their managers. The new politician was intensely interested in the poor and disadvantaged. His constituents were people from the same background as he was, and this identification deepened the dedication of Lionel Conacher MPP.

Conacher's early political career spanned years of tremendous importance in the history of this country and of the world. One year before his election to the provincial parliament, the federal government closed the Depression-era relief camps. The worst year of drought in the Prairies, 1937, was still to come. There were rapid changes occurring in the world situation that greatly affected Canada during the late 1930s and early 1940s. The Dominion built stronger bonds with the United States in 1936, when President Franklin D. Roosevelt visited Lord Tweedsmuir at the Citadel, Quebec. It was the first official visit of an American president to a governor general of Canada. Two years later there was the joint dedication of the Thousand Islands bridge by

*Proud and optimistic, the First Canadian Overseas Division embarked for England on December 18, 1939. How did Canada's involvement in World War II compare with her role in World War I?*

the two countries, and President Roosevelt promised armed assistance to Canada in the event of an invasion.

In Europe the Munich Agreement was signed on September 29, 1938, in an attempt to stop German aggression. In 1939 the United States and Canada entered into a new, three-year trade agreement, and King George VI and Queen Elizabeth toured the two countries. Canada was still feeling the effects of the 1937 General Motors strike in Oshawa, Ontario, and the lowest birthrate year in her history when German forces invaded Poland on September 1, 1939. Two days later England and France declared war on Germany, and on September 10 Canada entered the war. The War Measures Act, which gave the government absolute power if it considered the security of the nation threatened, was soon enacted.

The world conflict had been predicted throughout the 1930s, as Adolf Hitler rose to power. The 1936 Olympics held in Berlin were a symbol of Germany's national power, pride and political intentions. Hitler used the Olympics as a Nazi showcase, while he

*RCAF Squadron Leader Lionel Conacher during an officers course in Lachine, Quebec, 1942*

continued to build ships and increase war supplies and weaponry. When war broke out, Canada became an overseas source of war production for Britain. Eventually, Canadian troops distinguished themselves at the front as the nation was relied upon more and more in the total war effort.

The start of World War II brought Lionel Conacher — and many other Canadians — a new phase in his career. He was made an honorary squadron leader in the Royal Canadian Air Force. Before his officer's training course Conacher was sent by the federal government on a tour of Canada to help establish a sports program for the armed services. Conacher focussed his attention on improving the morale and fitness of the men he worked with. He oversaw the organization of sports leagues and benefit games. Lionel and Charlie once led a group of "oldtimers" in a benefit that raised $12 000 for the Navy League of Canada.

There was other business that attracted Conacher. In the late 1930s and early 1940s Lionel was one of the initial investors in the Turner Valley oil field in Alberta.

*Oil drillers in Alberta's Turner Valley, May 1914. Of what significance was the discovery of oil in this area? Why did it take from 1914 to the late 1930s for Turner Valley to attract substantial investments from people such as Lionel Conacher?*

He and Charlie had been advised to invest in the area by their immensely wealthy friend Max Bell. Combined with Lionel's stock market business and assets, the profits from this thriving oil interest guaranteed him financial success.

When he was not engaged in business pursuits, political activities, the Royal Canadian Air Force or benefit sporting events, Conacher immersed himself in the two favourite leisure pastimes of his later life. He was an eager reader of any book on the life and career of Napoleon Bonaparte. Conacher's interest in the "Little General" was well known, and his library of Napoleonic books was greatly increased when the father of his best friend, Jack Purcell, world-renowned badminton player, died and left Conacher his collection in his will.

Even more intense was Conacher's interest in hunting and fishing. Lionel and his wife often went on hunting trips with friends, including Mr. and Mrs. Jack Purcell and the Hon. Charles Box and Mrs. Box. Their trips took them to Port Arthur (now Thunder Bay), Ontario, in pursuit of partridge or to an area north of Portage La Prairie, Manitoba, for fowl. Lionel was a crack marksman with a twelve-gauge shotgun, and he spent many hours in duck blinds with his favourite dog, Mink. His only other retreat was in the Muskoka region of Cedar Point. Conacher bought a long strip of beach and land there, where he built three magnificent cedar log cottages. Quiet summers were spent at Cedar Point with his wife, daughters Connie and Diane, sons Lionel Junior, Brian and David and with his own brothers and sisters.

In 1943 Lionel received a shock at the nomination meeting in Bracondale. He was passed over for the Liberal nomination. Perhaps Conacher's various efforts during the war had lessened his effectiveness in his own riding. Not one to fret, Lionel immersed himself in business and family interests and made plans to try for a federal nomination. Two years later he was named the Liberal candidate in the federal riding of Trinity for the 1945 election. But like Bracondale, Trinity was traditionally a Conservative riding, and Conacher was unable to gather enough votes to win. However, as always, kept trying. Finally, in 1949, he did win the federal seat, which he captured again in the election of

*In 1943 Conacher was the director of the Ontario Athletic Commission.*

1953 with an increased popular vote.

Similar to his provincial political career, Conacher's federal parliamentary life was not high profile. He remained a contributing member of various committees and a conscientious backbencher who understood the importance of regular attendance in the House of Commons and of service to his constituents. On one occasion the leader of the Social Credit Party, Solon Low, introduced in the House a 1935 Conservative campaign pamphlet with a foreword by Lionel Conacher. He then asked what the Trinity MP was doing on the Liberal benches. Conacher, in the spirit of the question, replied, "That was before I grew up."

*Conacher and his favourite
hunting dog, Mink*

In 1950 Canadian Press staffwriter Jack Sullivan
organized a nationwide, twenty-two-question poll
designed to select and pay tribute to outstanding athletes
in the 1900 to 1950 period. The selections were made by
forty-three sportswriters and sportscasters across the
country. They were asked to name the greatest athlete of

the period in football, basketball, golf, hockey, lacrosse, rowing, soccer, swimming, tennis and track and field. They were to select the best basketball team, hockey team, lacrosse team, football team and soccer team and were to pinpoint the most dramatic sports event, the biggest upset and the most significant sports trend. Two other categories to be decided were the greatest female athlete and the greatest male athlete of the half-century.

Newspapers across Canada carried the daily announcements as they were released between December 20 and December 31, 1950. Track and field star Fanny "Bobby" Rosenfeld was elected the greatest female athlete by one vote over figure-skating sensation Barbara Ann Scott. The last Canadian Press announcement, presumably the highest honour, was the name of the greatest male athlete of the period. Lionel Conacher won with thirty-three votes, an overwhelming majority. Thirty-one votes behind, tied for second place, were Percy Williams, Vancouver sprinter and double gold medallist in the 1928 Olympics, and Harvey Pulford, Ottawa team sport sensation of the early 1900s. Significantly, in the same poll Conacher was chosen as the greatest football player of the past fifty years and received votes as the greatest lacrosse player (a title won by Newsy Lalonde).

The impressive title of greatest athlete of the half-century simply confirmed what had been known for a long time. In the House of Commons the Rev. Dan McIvor, MP for Fort William, said on March 8, 1951, that it "was an honour to the House that one of its members should be hailed across Canada as the greatest athlete of our times." Conacher replied from the floor:

It was very kind of the honourable member to bring to the attention of the House the fact that I was awarded this mythical title covering the last fifty years in sport. I realize that this House has before it too many important problems to be concerned with such matters as this. However, I should like to say that I believe that sport has its proper place in our way of life and that while overdone in many instances, it has served a useful purpose, particularly among the younger generation as it helps them develop their bodies: and a healthy body, I am sure we all agree, develops a healthy mind.

I should like to say that in the last fifty years I have played with and against many great teams and on more occasions than one I was in the position of either starting or helping to stop the attack. In my present position in this House, I have been relegated to the bench in a sense: but I feel quite satisfied with this position on such a fine team as we have here, which is quite capable of carrying the heavy burden placed on its shoulders in these trying days.

*What trophy is now awarded annually to Canada's most outstanding male athlete? Who are some of the athletes to have received this trophy?*

*Track and field star Bobby Rosenfeld. What professional sports do women play? Why are there fewer professional sports available to women?*

Who would you select as the
greatest Canadian athlete of the
past twenty-five years?

Sport was the context of Lionel Conacher's entire life.
It was through sport that he had entered politics, and
one of his objectives, among many others, had been to
funnel government aid to community parks in the
poorer districts of Toronto. In 1951 he became president
of the National Hockey League Oldtimers Association, a
group that used their athletic talents to help charities.
These retired hockey players left their jobs and
businesses many times a year to travel throughout
southern and eastern Ontario and into Quebec, reliving
their past hockey glory for the benefit of crippled
children or other worthy causes. In the three years that
Conacher was president, more than $60 000 was raised.
The association and its charity work still thrive today.

Lionel Conacher died much the way he had lived. In
late May 1954, at the annual Parliament-press softball
game on the lawn of Parliament Hill, Lionel Conacher
hit a high ball into right field. It disappeared into the
crowd. What normally would have been a single was
stretched into a triple. Conacher ran to third base
without slowing down. Suddenly, he collapsed. Twenty
minutes later he was pronounced dead of a heart attack.
Shock and disbelief struck everyone who heard the
news; tributes poured in from all parts of Canada. Prime
Minister Louis St. Laurent spoke for all when he stated:

The news of his passing will be met with the deepest sorrow by his
colleagues in Parliament, by those whom he represented in Ottawa
and by all sports-loving Canadians. No matter what task he
undertook, it was typical of Lionel Conacher that he devoted his
energy to it.

St. John's Anglican Church in York Mills was filled to
capacity as seven hundred mourners gathered inside for
the funeral service. Hundreds more filed through to pay
their last respects after the family service. The press
recorded: "Then the body was borne slowly to the
flower-banked chancel of St. John's, where thousands
were waiting to file past the casket of this legendary
figure."

It was a scene befitting a national hero. Honorary
pallbearers from federal, provincial and municipal
governments, from the business and sporting
communities and from Conacher's family sat or stood
amid abundant and colourful floral tributes. The flowers
ranged from very elaborate arrangements — a huge

## Further Reading

Batten, Jack. *Champions.* Toronto: New Press, 1971.

Cosentino, Frank. *Ned Hanlan.* Don Mills, Ont.: Fitzhenry & Whiteside, 1978.

Cosentino, Frank and Glynn Leshon. *Olympic Gold: Canada's Winners in the Summer Games.* Toronto: Holt, Rinehart and Winston, 1975.

Frayne, Trent. "The Clan Conacher" in *The Mad Men of Hockey.* Toronto: McClelland and Stewart, 1974.

Howell, Max and Nancy Howell. *Sports and Games in Canadian Life.* Toronto: Macmillan, 1969.

Kidd, Bruce. *Tom Longboat.* Don Mills, Ont.: Fitzhenry & Whiteside, 1980.

Morrow, Don. "Lionel Pretoria Conacher." *Journal of Sport History,* Vol. 6, No. 1 (1979), pp. 5-37.

Roxborough, Henry. *One Hundred — Not Out: The Story of Nineteenth-Century Canadian Sport.* Toronto: Ryerson, 1966.

Whitehead, Eric. *Cyclone Taylor: A Hockey Legend.* Toronto: Doubleday, 1977.

Wise, S.F. and Douglas Fisher. *Canada's Sporting Heroes.* Toronto: General, 1974.

## Credits

The authors would like to thank the Conacher family and relatives, especially Victoria Mayhue and Constance Murphy, for their complete cooperation in providing records and information. To our families, thank you for your support. Special thanks to Mrs. Gail Smith for her typing.

Every effort has been made to credit all sources correctly. The author and publishers will welcome any information that will allow them to correct any errors or omissions.

The publishers wish to express their gratitude to the following who have given permission to use copyrighted illustrations in this book:

Alexandra Studio/Canada's Sports Hall of Fame, 43, 45

Archives of Alberta, 57

Canada's Sports Hall of Fame, cover, 11, 19, 21, 22, 29, 41

Canadian Press, 63

Charles Templeton, 48

Hockey Hall of Fame, 25

Mrs. Victoria Mayhue, frontispiece, 9, 13, 14, 15, 17, 26, 35, 42, 46, 49, 50, 52, 54, 56, 59, 60

Ontario Archives, 4

Pennsylvania State Archives, 23(MG-213, Postcard Collection)

Public Archives of Canada, 33(C-24840), 38(C-1959), 55(C-24717), 61

Toronto Archives (James Collection), 3, 5, 7, 27

Toronto *Star,* 37

Toronto *Sun* 31

## Index

*Lionel Conacher and three other Liberal MPs watch from the bench during a Parliament-press softball game in the early 1950s.*

basket of red roses from the Montreal Canadiens — to a simple, yet eloquent bouquet sent "to a friend from a friend". As the funeral cortege left St. John's for burial in the churchyard, the hushed assembly followed in respect. A poem published in 1922 seemed appropriate that day in 1954:

Whose football play is as a dream
Of speed and strength in the extreme?
Who constitutes the Argo team?
  Conacher.

Whose hockey playing is immense?
Who plays with skill and yet sense,
And never decorates the fence?
  Conacher.

A baseball player out and out
Of that there is no idle doubt.
What would the Hillcrests do without
  Conacher?

He plays a star game of lacrosse
And very rarely suffers loss.
Say! Who at all the games is boss?
  Conacher.

Who always does the best he can
To play the game and please the fan?
Who is the champion and all-round man?
  Conacher.